delicious
diabetic
recipes

W9-BJF-824

Savory Soups & Stews

savory
soups & stews

Sweet Potato Stew

- 1 cup chopped onion
- 1 cup chopped celery
- 1 cup grated peeled sweet potato
- 1 cup reduced-sodium vegetable broth or water
- 2 slices bacon, crisp-cooked and crumbled
- 1 cup fat-free half-and-half
  Black pepper
- ¼ cup minced fresh parsley

SLOW COOKER DIRECTIONS

1. Place onion, celery, sweet potato, broth and bacon in slow cooker. Cover; cook on LOW 6 hours or until vegetables are tender.

2. Increase heat to HIGH. Stir in half-and-half. Add water, if needed, to reach desired consistency. Cook, uncovered, 30 minutes on HIGH or until heated through.

3. Season to taste with pepper. Stir in parsley.

Makes 4 servings

Nutrients per Serving: 1½ cups stew
Calories: 112, **Calories from Fat:** 13%, **Total Fat:** 2g,
Saturated Fat: <1g, **Cholesterol:** 13mg, **Sodium:** 280mg,
Carbohydrate: 18g, **Fiber:** 2g, **Protein:** 5g

Dietary Exchanges: 1 Starch

Chilled Cucumber Soup

1 large cucumber, peeled and coarsely chopped
¾ cup reduced-fat sour cream
¼ cup packed fresh dill
½ teaspoon salt (optional)
⅛ teaspoon ground white pepper (optional)
1½ cups fat-free reduced-sodium chicken or vegetable broth
4 fresh dill sprigs

1. Place cucumber in food processor; process until finely chopped. Add sour cream, ¼ cup dill, salt and pepper, if desired; process until smooth.

2. Transfer mixture to large bowl; stir in broth. Cover and chill at least 2 hours or up to 24 hours. Ladle into shallow bowls; garnish with dill sprigs.

Makes 4 servings

Nutrients per Serving: ¾ cup soup
Calories: 67, **Calories from Fat:** 54%, **Total Fat:** 4g,
Saturated Fat: 2g, **Cholesterol:** 13mg, **Sodium:** 236mg,
Carbohydrate: 6g, **Fiber:** <1g, **Protein:** 3g

Dietary Exchanges: 1 Fat

tip

Whole cucumbers may be stored in the vegetable drawer of the refrigerator for up to one week. Cut cucumbers, securely wrapped in plastic wrap, may be refrigerated for two to three days.

Chicken and Chile Pepper Stew

1 pound boneless skinless chicken thighs,
  cut into ½-inch pieces
1 pound small potatoes, sliced
1 cup chopped onion
2 poblano peppers, seeded and diced
1 jalapeño pepper,* seeded and finely chopped
3 cloves garlic, minced
3 cups fat-free reduced-sodium chicken broth
1 can (about 14 ounces) no-salt-added diced tomatoes
2 tablespoons chili powder
1 teaspoon dried oregano

Jalapeño peppers can sting and irritate the skin, so wear rubber gloves when handling peppers and do not touch your eyes.

SLOW COOKER DIRECTIONS

1. Place chicken, potatoes, onion, poblano peppers, jalapeño pepper and garlic in slow cooker.

2. Combine broth, tomatoes, chili powder and oregano in large bowl. Pour broth mixture over chicken mixture in slow cooker; mix well. Cover; cook on LOW 8 to 9 hours.

Makes 6 servings

Nutrients per Serving: ⅙ of total recipe
Calories: 257, **Calories from Fat:** 27%, **Total Fat:** 8g,
Saturated Fat: 2g, **Cholesterol:** 68mg, **Sodium:** 223mg,
Carbohydrate: 23g, **Fiber:** 4g, **Protein:** 25g

Dietary Exchanges: ½ Starch, 3 Meat, 1½ Fat

Mediterranean Fish Soup

4 ounces uncooked pastina or other small pasta
¾ cup chopped onion
2 cloves garlic, minced
1 teaspoon whole fennel seeds
1 can (about 14 ounces) no-salt-added stewed tomatoes
1 can (about 14 ounces) fat-free reduced-sodium chicken broth
1 tablespoon minced fresh parsley
½ teaspoon black pepper
¼ teaspoon ground turmeric
8 ounces firm white fish, cut into 1-inch pieces
3 ounces uncooked small shrimp, peeled and deveined

1. Cook pasta according to package directions, omitting salt. Drain; set aside.

2. Spray large nonstick saucepan with nonstick cooking spray. Add onion, garlic and fennel seeds; cook and stir over medium heat 3 minutes or until onion is tender.

3. Stir in tomatoes, broth, parsley, pepper and turmeric. Bring to a boil; reduce heat and simmer 10 minutes. Add fish; cook 1 minute. Add shrimp; cook until shrimp are pink and opaque.

4. Divide pasta among 4 bowls; ladle soup over pasta.

Makes 4 servings

Nutrients per Serving: 1½ cups soup with ½ cup cooked pasta
Calories: 209, **Calories from Fat:** 10%, **Total Fat:** 2g,
Saturated Fat: <1g, **Cholesterol:** 59mg, **Sodium:** 111mg,
Carbohydrate: 28g, **Fiber:** 3g, **Protein:** 19g

Dietary Exchanges: 2 Starch, 2 Meat

Butternut Squash Soup

2 teaspoons olive oil
1 large sweet onion, chopped
1 medium red bell pepper, chopped
2 packages (10 ounces each) frozen puréed butternut
     squash, thawed
1 can (10¾ ounces) condensed reduced-sodium
     chicken broth, undiluted
¼ teaspoon ground nutmeg
⅛ teaspoon ground white pepper
½ cup fat-free half-and-half

1. Heat oil in large saucepan over medium-high heat. Add onion and bell pepper; cook and stir 5 minutes. Add squash, broth, nutmeg and white pepper; bring to a boil over high heat. Reduce heat; cover and simmer about 15 minutes or until vegetables are very tender.

2. Purée soup in saucepan with hand-held immersion blender or in batches in food processor or blender. Return soup to saucepan. Stir in half-and-half; heat through. Add additional half-and-half, if necessary, to thin soup to desired consistency.

Makes 4 servings

Serving Suggestion: Garnish with a swirl of fat-free half-and-half or a sprinkling of fresh parsley.

Nutrients per Serving: 1½ cups soup
Calories: 152, **Calories from Fat:** 17%, **Total Fat:** 3g,
Saturated Fat: 1g, **Cholesterol:** 13mg, **Sodium:** 155mg,
Carbohydrate: 28g, **Fiber:** 3g, **Protein:** 6g

Dietary Exchanges: 2 Starch, ½ Fat

Summer's Best Gazpacho

3 cups reduced-sodium tomato juice
2½ cups finely diced tomatoes (about 2 large)
1 cup finely diced yellow or red bell pepper (1 small)
1 cup finely diced unpeeled cucumber
½ cup chunky salsa
1 tablespoon olive oil
1 clove garlic, minced
1 ripe avocado, diced
¼ cup finely chopped cilantro or basil

1. Combine tomato juice, tomatoes, bell pepper, cucumber, salsa, oil and garlic in large bowl; mix well.

2. Cover and refrigerate at least 1 hour or up to 24 hours before serving. Stir in avocado and cilantro just before serving.

Makes 6 servings

Nutrients per Serving: 1¼ cups soup
Calories: 127, **Calories from Fat:** 57%, **Total Fat:** 8g,
Saturated Fat: 1g, **Cholesterol:** 0mg, **Sodium:** 444mg,
Carbohydrate: 15g, **Fiber:** 4g, **Protein:** 4g

Dietary Exchanges: 1 Starch, 1½ Fat

Moroccan Lentil & Vegetable Soup

1 tablespoon olive oil
1 cup chopped onion
4 cloves garlic, minced
½ cup dried lentils, rinsed, sorted and drained
1½ teaspoons ground coriander
1½ teaspoons ground cumin
½ teaspoon ground cinnamon
½ teaspoon black pepper
3¾ cups fat-free reduced-sodium chicken or vegetable broth
½ cup chopped celery
½ cup chopped sun-dried tomatoes (not packed in oil)
1 yellow squash, chopped
½ cup chopped green bell pepper
1 cup chopped plum tomatoes
½ cup chopped fresh parsley
¼ cup chopped fresh cilantro or basil

1. Heat oil in medium saucepan over medium-high heat. Add onion and garlic; cook and stir 4 minutes or until onion is tender. Stir in lentils, coriander, cumin, cinnamon and black pepper; cook 2 minutes. Add broth, celery and sun-dried tomatoes; bring to a boil. Reduce heat to medium-low; cover and simmer 25 minutes.

2. Stir in squash and bell pepper. Cover and cook 10 minutes or until lentils are tender.

3. Top with plum tomatoes, parsley and cilantro just before serving. *Makes 6 servings*

Nutrients per Serving: 1 cup soup
Calories: 131, **Calories from Fat:** 20%, **Total Fat:** 3g,
Saturated Fat: <1g, **Cholesterol:** 0mg, **Sodium:** 264mg,
Carbohydrate: 20g, **Fiber:** 2g, **Protein:** 8g

Dietary Exchanges: 1 Vegetable, 1 Starch, ½ Fat

Beef Goulash Soup with Caraway

1¼ pounds boneless beef sirloin tri-tip roast*
1 teaspoon canola oil
1 cup chopped onion
3 cans (about 14 ounces each) reduced-sodium beef broth
2 cans (about 14 ounces each) diced tomatoes, undrained
1½ cups sliced carrots
2 tablespoons sugar
1 tablespoon paprika
1 tablespoon caraway seeds, slightly crushed
2 cloves garlic, minced
4 ounces (about 2 cups) uncooked whole wheat egg noodles
2 cups thinly sliced cabbage**

Substitute chuck roast or beef round steak, if desired.

**Substitute 2 cups packaged coleslaw mix, if desired.*

1. Trim fat from beef and discard. Cut beef into 1-inch pieces. Heat oil in large nonstick saucepan over medium heat. Brown beef in 2 batches; transfer to paper towel-lined plate. Drain fat from saucepan. Return beef to saucepan. Add onion; cook and stir about 3 minutes or until onion is tender.

2. Add broth, tomatoes, carrots, sugar, paprika, caraway seeds and garlic. Bring to a boil. Reduce heat; cover and simmer about 45 minutes or until beef is tender.

3. Stir in noodles. Return to a boil. Reduce heat; simmer, uncovered, about 10 minutes or until noodles are tender. Stir in cabbage. Cook 1 to 2 minutes more or until heated through. *Makes 8 to 9 servings*

Nutrients per Serving: 1 cup soup
Calories: 235, **Calories from Fat:** 19%, **Total Fat:** 5g, **Saturated Fat:** 1g, **Cholesterol:** 26mg, **Sodium:** 273mg, **Carbohydrate:** 27g, **Fiber:** 4g, **Protein:** 22g

Dietary Exchanges: 2 Starch, 2 Meat, 1 Fat

Vietnamese Beef and Noodle Soup

4 cups water
2 ounces whole wheat spaghetti, broken in half
2¼ cups reduced-fat reduced-sodium beef broth
1 shallot, sliced
1 whole star anise*
½ teaspoon minced fresh ginger
1 teaspoon fish sauce or reduced-sodium soy sauce
1 teaspoon reduced-sodium soy sauce
½ teaspoon hot pepper sauce
6 ounces boneless beef sirloin, sliced ⅛ inch thick
⅛ teaspoon salt
⅛ teaspoon black pepper
1 cup bean sprouts
2 green onions, thinly sliced
1 small fresh red chile pepper, thinly sliced
2 lime wedges
2 tablespoons fresh cilantro leaves

*Star anise is a star-shaped, dark brown pod used in many Asian cuisines. It can be found in Asian markets or the spice section of some grocery stores.

1. Bring water to a boil in medium saucepan. Add pasta; cook 3 to 4 minutes or until tender. Drain. Bring broth, shallot, star anise and ginger to a boil in medium saucepan. Reduce heat; simmer 10 minutes. Strain liquid into large saucepan; discard solids. Stir in fish sauce, soy sauce and hot pepper sauce.

2. Season beef with salt and black pepper. Add beef and bean sprouts to broth mixture; cook 1 to 2 minutes or until beef is no longer pink. Stir in cooked pasta and green onions. Ladle soup into 2 bowls; top with chile slices, lime juice and cilantro.

Makes 2 servings

Nutrients per Serving: ½ of total recipe
Calories: 258, **Calories from Fat:** 21%, **Total Fat:** 6g,
Saturated Fat: 2g, **Cholesterol:** 40mg, **Sodium:** 515mg,
Carbohydrate: 27g, **Fiber:** 5g, **Protein:** 23g

Dietary Exchanges: 2 Starch, 2 Meat

Mediterranean Soup with Mozzarella

2 medium green bell peppers, chopped
1 cup chopped yellow onion
2 cups (about 8 ounces) chopped eggplant
1 cup (about 4 ounces) sliced mushrooms
2 cloves garlic, minced
2 tablespoons dried basil, divided
3 cups water
1 can (about 14 ounces) diced tomatoes with Italian
    herbs, undrained
½ cup red wine or water
1 can (about 15 ounces) no-salt-added white beans,
    rinsed and drained
2 teaspoons sugar
¼ teaspoon salt
1½ cups (6 ounces) shredded reduced-fat mozzarella
    cheese
¼ cups minced fresh parsley

1. Spray large saucepan with nonstick cooking spray. Heat over medium-high heat. Add bell peppers and onion; cook and stir 4 minutes or until onion is translucent.

2. Add eggplant, mushrooms, garlic and all but 1 teaspoon basil; cook and stir 4 minutes. Stir in water, tomatoes and wine. Reduce heat; cover and simmer 30 minutes, stirring occasionally.

3. Remove saucepan from heat. Stir in beans, sugar and salt. Cover; let stand 5 minutes. Combine remaining 1 teaspoon basil, parsley and cheese. Top each serving with ¼ cup cheese mixture. *Makes 6 servings*

Nutrients per Serving: 1¼ cups with ¼ cup cheese topping
Calories: 130, **Calories from Fat:** 22%, **Total Fat:** 3g,
Saturated Fat: 1g, **Cholesterol:** 3mg, **Sodium:** 411mg,
Carbohydrate: 9g, **Fiber:** 2g, **Protein:** 16g

Dietary Exchanges: 1 Vegetable, 2 Lean Meat, ½ Starch, ½ Fat

Chunky Chicken Stew

1 teaspoon olive oil
1 small onion, chopped
1 cup thinly sliced carrots
1 cup fat-free reduced-sodium chicken broth
1 can (about 14 ounces) no-salt-added diced tomatoes
1 cup diced cooked chicken breast
3 cups sliced kale or baby spinach

1. Heat oil in large saucepan over medium-high heat. Add onion; cook and stir about 5 minutes or until golden brown. Stir in carrots and broth; bring to a boil. Reduce heat; simmer, uncovered, 5 minutes. Add tomatoes; simmer 5 minutes more or until carrots are tender.

2. Add chicken; cook and stir until heated through. Add kale, stirring until wilted. Simmer 1 minute.   *Makes 2 servings*

Nutrients per Serving: ½ of total recipe
Calories: 287, **Calories from Fat:** 18%, **Total Fat:** 6g,
Saturated Fat: 1g, **Cholesterol:** 66mg, **Sodium:** 337mg,
Carbohydrate: 30g, **Fiber:** 8g, **Protein:** 30g

Dietary Exchanges: 6 Vegetable, 3 Meat, 1 Fat

Broccoli Cream Soup with Green Onions

1 tablespoon olive oil
2 cups chopped onions
1 pound fresh or frozen broccoli florets or spears
2 cups reduced-sodium chicken or vegetable broth
6 tablespoons reduced-fat cream cheese
1 cup fat-free (skim) milk
¾ teaspoon salt (optional)
⅛ teaspoon ground red pepper
⅓ cup finely chopped green onions

1. Heat oil in large saucepan over medium-high heat. Add onions; cook and stir 4 minutes or until translucent.

2. Add broccoli and broth to saucepan; bring to a boil over high heat. Reduce heat; cover and simmer 10 minutes or until broccoli is tender.

3. Working in batches, process mixture in food processor or blender until smooth. Return mixture to saucepan over medium heat. Whisk in cream cheese until melted. Stir in milk, salt, if desired, and red pepper. Cook 2 minutes or until heated through. Top with green onions. *Makes 5 servings*

Nutrients per Serving: 1 cup soup
Calories: 115, **Calories from Fat:** 24%, **Total Fat:** 4g,
Saturated Fat: 2g, **Cholesterol:** 10mg, **Sodium:** 569mg,
Carbohydrate: 16g, **Fiber:** 4g, **Protein:** 7g

Dietary Exchanges: 1 Starch, 1 Fat

Kansas City Steak Soup

8 ounces ground beef
3 cups frozen mixed vegetables
2 cups water
1 can (about 14 ounces) stewed tomatoes, undrained
1 cup chopped onion
1 cup sliced celery
1 beef bouillon cube
½ to 1 teaspoon black pepper
1 can (about 14 ounces) reduced-sodium beef broth
½ cup all-purpose flour

1. Brown beef in large saucepan over medium-high heat 6 to 8 minutes, stirring to break up meat. Drain fat.

2. Add mixed vegetables, water, tomatoes, onion, celery, bouillon cube and pepper to saucepan; bring to a boil.

3. Whisk broth and flour in small bowl until smooth; add to beef mixture, stirring constantly. Return mixture to a boil. Reduce heat to low; cover and simmer 15 minutes, stirring frequently.

Makes 6 servings

Note: If time permits, allow the soup to simmer an additional 30 minutes to allow the flavors to blend.

Nutrients per Serving: 1⅔ cups soup
Calories: 198, **Calories from Fat:** 23%, **Total Fat:** 5g,
Saturated Fat: 2g, **Cholesterol:** 23mg, **Sodium:** 598mg,
Carbohydrate: 27g, **Fiber:** 5g, **Protein:** 13g

Dietary Exchanges: 3½ Vegetable, ½ Starch, 1 Meat, 1 Fat

Smoky Navy Bean Soup

2½ tablespoons olive oil, divided
4 ounces Canadian bacon or extra-lean ham, diced
1 cup diced onion
1 large carrot, thinly sliced
1 stalk celery, thinly sliced
3 cups water
6 ounces red potatoes, diced
2 bay leaves
¼ teaspoon dried tarragon
1 can (about 15 ounces) navy beans, rinsed and drained
1½ teaspoons liquid smoke
½ teaspoon salt (optional)
½ teaspoon black pepper

1. Heat 1 tablespoon oil in large saucepan over medium-high heat. Add bacon; cook and stir 2 minutes or until browned. Remove bacon to paper towel-lined plate.

2. Add onion, carrot and celery to saucepan; spray with nonstick cooking spray. Cook and stir 4 minutes or until onion is translucent. Add water; bring to a boil over high heat. Add potatoes, bay leaves and tarragon; return to a boil. Reduce heat; cover and simmer 20 minutes or until potatoes are tender. Remove from heat.

3. Stir in beans, bacon, remaining 1½ tablespoons oil, liquid smoke, salt, if desired, and pepper. Remove and discard bay leaves before serving. *Makes 6 servings*

Nutrients per Serving: 1 cup soup
Calories: 177, **Calories from Fat:** 26%, **Total Fat:** 5g,
Saturated Fat: <1g, **Cholesterol:** 9mg, **Sodium:** 599mg,
Carbohydrate: 23g, **Fiber:** 5g, **Protein:** 10g

Dietary Exchanges: ½ Starch, 1 Meat, 1 Fat